Nature's Super Secrets

How Do Seeds Sprout?

By Evan Rhodes

 **Gareth Stevens**
Publishing

Please visit our website, www.garethstevens.com. For a free color catalog of all our high-quality books, call toll free 1-800-542-2595 or fax 1-877-542-2596.

Library of Congress Cataloging-in-Publication Data

Rhodes, Evan.
 How do seeds sprout? / Evan Rhodes.
     p. cm. – (Nature's super secrets)
 Includes index.
 ISBN 978-1-4339-8166-1 (pbk.)
 ISBN 978-1-4339-8167-8 (6-pack)
 ISBN 978-1-4339-8165-4 (library binding)
 1. Germination—Juvenile literature. 2. Seeds—Juvenile literature. I. Title. II. Series:
Rhodes, Evan. Nature's super secrets.
 QK740.R485 2013
 571.8'62—dc23

                                        2012030513

Published in 2013 by
Gareth Stevens Publishing
111 East 14th Street, Suite 349
New York, NY 10003

Designer: Michael J. Flynn
Editor: Sarah Machajewski

Photo credits: Cover isak55/Shutterstock.com; p. 5 Geanina Bechea/Shutterstock.com; p. 7 Chepko Danil Vitalevich/Shutterstock.com; p. 9 Ariel Bravy/Shutterstock.com; p. 11 Velychko/Shutterstock.com; p. 13 rlat/Shutterstock.com; p. 15 Bogdan Wankowicz/Shutterstock.com; p. 17 Richard Griffin/Shutterstock.com; p. 19 ER_09/Shutterstock.com; p. 21 HABRDA/Shutterstock.com.

Printed in the United States of America

CPSIA compliance information: Batch #CW13GS: For further information contact Gareth Stevens, New York, New York at 1-800-542-2595.

Table of Contents

Boldface words appear in the glossary.

Tiny Plants

Our world has many kinds of plants, such as flowers, trees, and grass. They look different, but they all start out as seeds. Inside every seed, there's a tiny plant waiting to grow!

All seeds come from full-grown plants. Sometimes, animals and wind carry seeds to different places. We can also buy seeds from the store. We plant them in the ground or in a pot.

7

Inside a Seed

Seeds have all the parts a plant needs to grow. They have little **roots** and leaves. They also have a **seed coat**. The seed coat is like a hard shell. It keeps the plant safe from bugs, people, and the weather.

seed coat

Seeds have food inside them, too. Baby plants use the food until they sprout. Sprouting is when something starts to grow. It happens a few days after the seeds are planted. Do you know what seeds need to sprout?

Water, Air, and Sun

All seeds need water. Water makes the seeds soft and helps open the seed coat. Seeds need air and sun, too. They get these things even though they're covered with dirt! The dirt also gives them **nutrients**.

Finally, seeds need warmth. That's why most plants grow in the spring and summer. After a few days, seeds begin to sprout. This happens under the ground. We can't see them yet, but we will soon!

15

Sprouting

First, the baby plant grows roots.
The roots grow deep into the dirt.
They help the plant take in water
and stay in the ground. Some
plants have many little roots.
Other plants have one long root.

Next, the **stem** grows. It grows toward the light. In a few days, it comes above the ground. The stem helps the plant stand up and makes it short or tall. Some plants grow flowers and leaves from their stem.

Baby Seed, Adult Plant

Plants make seeds when they become adults. The new seeds sprout and make new plants. They look just like the plants they came from. It's fun watching plants grow. They make our world pretty!

How a Plant Grows

1

The seed
is planted.

2

The seed gets
sun and water.

3

The seed sprouts.

4

The plant comes
above the dirt.

5

The plant grows
leaves and flowers.

6

The plant
makes seeds.

Glossary

nutrient: something a living thing needs to grow and stay alive

root: the part of a plant that grows underground

seed coat: the hard outer shell of a seed

stem: one part of a plant that grows above the ground

For More Information

Books

Kim, Sue. *How Does a Seed Grow?* New York, NY: Little Simon, 2010.

Salas, Laura Purdie. *From Seed to Daisy: Following the Life Cycle.* Bloomington, MN: Picture Window Books, 2009.

Websites

All About Seeds

seeds.sciencenetlinks.com/seeds/
Learn fun facts and view photos of different kinds of seeds.

Biology of Plants: Starting to Grow

www.mbgnet.net/bioplants/grow.html
Read about where plants come from and view a video of a seed sprouting!

Grow Plant

www.cookie.com/kids/games/grow-plant.html
Learn about a plant's life cycle with this interactive website.

Index